How To Find Your Soulmate

The Wrong Way To Find Your Soulmate Online The
Humorous Women's Guide To Avoiding The Risks
Of Online Dating Scams

*(How To Use Smart Dating Strategies To Attract The Man
Of Your Dreams)*

Wallace Stewart

TABLE OF CONTENT

Engage In Mutual Interests And Pastimes............1

What Are The Defining Characteristics Of A Healthy Relationship? 23

Characteristics In Females Disliked By Males 41

Heal Your Body..55

The Correlation Between Achieving Success And Its Impact On The Search For A Life Partner. 64

Online Dating And Communication.....................79

Engaging & Investing..96

The Emerging Frontier Of Online Dating.......102

How To Get The Man Of Your Dreams 134

Strategies For Achieving Your Ideal Female Self 145

Engage In Mutual Interests And Pastimes.

Having shared interests or commonalities is of great significance as it enhances the likelihood of fostering a connection and rapport with others.

As a consequence of this, there is an increased likelihood that you will be inclined towards individuals whose interests correspond with your own. Nevertheless, it is imperative not to feign interest in these matters, as their perception of insincerity will be immediate, potentially causing profound demotivation.

Make them laugh

If one desires to establish a lasting impression, the most effective approach entails evoking laughter from the individuals in question. This entails leveraging your comedic sensibility to evoke laughter from them.

It is often suggested that successful humor has the potential to elicit deep emotional connections that can foster romantic attachment. In order to ensure their enjoyment in your presence, why not share your most entertaining jokes and employ your finest punch lines?

Key Principles for Establishing Healthy Relationships in Every Partnership

Regardless of whether you are in the early stages of a relationship or have been together for an extended period of time, guidelines can assist in advancing it to a more advanced stage. Adhere to the subsequent instructions and behold the transformative effects take place:

1. Unconditional love: Love cannot be contingent upon any terms or requirements. The relationship becomes excessively materialistic when the presence of conditional statements begins to infiltrate.

The ability to love should not be contingent upon your spouse's income, regular gift-giving, or their constant physical appearance. Cherish your partner in the same manner that your parents cherish you - without condition.

2. Give priority to your relationship: Place utmost emphasis on nurturing your bond. Devote time and energy to nurturing your relationship, and make consistent endeavors to enhance it.

3. Maintain consistent availability for communication: Lack of communication can lead to the gradual dissolution of your relationship. Ensure that your discourse is characterized by transparency and candor. Regardless of your level of busyness or fatigue, do not allow these factors to impede your ability to communicate effectively.

4. Hug with regularity: Incorporate it into your daily regimen and prolong the embrace. Embracing increases the levels of oxytocin, commonly referred to as the hormone of love, and decreases the levels of cortisol, known as the hormone of stress.

5. Engage in intimate relationships liberally: Avoid scheduling encounters and instead embrace spontaneity. At that juncture, excitement ensues and a profound bond between individuals is fostered. Do not let any hindrances impede your participation in sexual activities.

6. Engage in meaningful shared experiences: It is not imperative that you partake in a formal outing. You could also opt to partake in a romantic dinner at your residence, ensuring relaxation in either the garden or balcony, where you can reminisce on cherished moments or

engage in the shared experience of watching your preferred television program. The objective is to carve out a respite from your demanding routines in order to maintain proximity.

7. To establish trust, it is imperative to be forthright and adhere to the principles of honesty and truthfulness. Trust is engendered through the foundation of integrity and transparency. Infidelity is categorically incompatible with the foundations of a committed partnership, although small and innocuous deceits may be permitted as a means of enhancing spousal contentment.

8. Offer a constructive and uplifting critique when seeking to improve your spouse, refraining from causing any harm in the process. Assist your partner in understanding the underlying intention behind the critique.

9. Engage in constructive discussions: Disagreements can be beneficial when they occur sporadically and without causing harm. Both parties can diplomatically maintain differing viewpoints. Cultivate the habit of attentive listening and engaging in fewer arguments. That demonstrates the level of mutual respect you have for one another.

10. Stand in solidarity: Although we hope that adversities will not disrupt your life, it is during these challenging moments that you must remain steadfastly committed to your partner, demonstrating unwavering love and support for one another. At that point, your connection becomes fortified.

11. Revel in the marvels present in your relationship: Irrespective of the simplicity or ordinariness of the tasks,

exhibit appreciation towards your partner and express gratitude for their efforts. It signifies your acknowledgment and admiration towards them, both of which are fundamental for establishing a enduring relationship.

12. Respect the need for personal space: Closeness should not be mistaken for emotional dependency on one's partner. Provide them with their own designated area, refrain from disturbing them for a certain period of time during the day, and allow them to unwind in a manner of their choosing. Likewise, ensure that you allocate ample time for personal endeavors, such as pursuing your professional goals, engaging in your hobbies, or simply unwinding and rejuvenating.

13. Honor significant milestones: Remember to acknowledge the important moments in your relationship,

such as the day of your initial encounter, your inaugural outing together, the occasion of your partner's proposal, as well as your respective birthdays and matrimonial anniversary. Commend your unity and forge unforgettable memories.

14. Comprehend and demonstrate empathy towards your partner: In the event that your significant other experiences severe agitation and directs their anger towards you, exercise self-restraint and abstain from reciprocating in a similar manner. They may have had a particularly challenging day at their job or been experiencing a significant amount of stress. Gain an understanding of their perspective, demonstrate empathy towards their feelings, and at an opportune time, ascertain the source of their distress.

15. Pardon and disregard: Errors are bound to occur. If you experience pain caused by your loved one, extend your forgiveness and release the memory of it. When you err, it will serve as an inspiration for them to follow suit.

16. Demonstrate genuine curiosity in your spouse's hobbies and activities: Is there a particular sport or pastime that your partner engages in that fails to captivate your interest? You need not disclose that information to them! Instead, endeavor to comprehend the sport, and engage your spouse in conversation regarding it. Express curiosity and actively participate in your partner's interests. In due course, you will develop an appreciation for them.

17. Inquire about your desires: It would be unrealistic to anticipate that your spouse will fully understand all of your needs and desires. Telepathic

communication may not consistently manifest. Should you require any assistance, do not hesitate to make your request.

18. Embrace the imperfections: No individual is without flaws! Welcome your partner unconditionally, embracing both their strengths and weaknesses. Successful relationships are built on being the suitable companion rather than the hypothetical companion, as perfection is unattainable.

19. Maintain your commitments: By doing so, you cultivate a sense of trustworthiness, reliability, and enhance your standing.

20. Strive for excellence and endeavor to reach your utmost potential: Each one of us is susceptible to critique and apprehension - the profound uneasiness

of committing mistakes and facing subsequent judgment. Exert your utmost efforts in nurturing your relationship, regardless of your partner's reaction or reciprocation. There is a limit to what one can do; the reaction of one's spouse is beyond one's control.

Before We Begin...

Although the answers generated should be original to you, there exist certain regulations that must be adhered to as you navigate through this book. Failure to comply with these guidelines will impede the attainment of your desired outcomes. If you are unable to provide consent to the terms outlined below, we kindly request that you refrain from further engagement with this material and revisit it at a later time when you are able to do so.

It is imperative that you maintain unwavering honesty with yourself, regardless of any circumstances. The intent of these questions and exercises is to assist you in discerning your areas of proficiency and areas for improvement, as well as identifying any anxieties or difficulties you may have encountered. One might discover the inclination to respond to these inquiries from the perspective of their future self, or as an individual they aspire to become. Nevertheless, it is crucial for you to reside in the present moment and provide responses to your inquiries based on your current circumstances.

It is imperative to respond to all inquiries, even if it necessitates extending the exercise beyond a single day. To put it succinctly, should you opt to skip any segment of this book or casually overlook these inquiries, it will undoubtedly pose challenges in subsequent exercises.

It is imperative that you follow a chronological progression while working through this book. Do not skip ahead. The compilation of these journals will ultimately result in the development of your ideal dating profile. It is imperative that you perform each exercise sequentially while allocating sufficient time for contemplation before composing your response. The greater quantity of content you are capable of producing, the more advantageous it will be for you in your pursuit of love.

It is imperative that you retain all of your journals until their completion. Regardless of whether you choose to respond using a ballpoint pen and composition book, or opt for digital platforms such as Evernote or a Word document, it is advised to consolidate all of your responses and archive them for future reference.

Given that we have established a shared understanding, you are now prepared to commence the program titled "Achieving

Success in Online Dating within a 7-Day Period."

Day 6: Prepared for Broadcasting

Today marks the occasion of your triumphant return to the online dating realm, armed with an impeccably refined profile. This marks a significant initial stride towards the desired outcome. Despite any previous setbacks or subpar outcomes you may have experienced in the realm of online dating, it is imperative that you afford yourself the opportunity to engage in this endeavor once again. By crafting a profile that effectively showcases your strengths and appealing qualities, devoid of any negativity or monotonous answers, you will discover a suitable match.

Moreover, albeit approaching it with a level of doubt, it is important to acknowledge that having the ability to clearly pinpoint your desires increases the probability of encountering precisely the individual you envision.

Recall the premise established at the onset of the book, wherein the likelihood of encountering a suitable partner is not contingent upon any particular dating platform or application. Select the one or two options for which you have a sense of ease, and align the components of your profile with the structure of those options. It might be necessary to revise or reorganize portions of the content, however, the fundamental principle of your message must remain unaltered.

Additionally, it is imperative to allocate sufficient time to address any inquiries that may be presented by the respective websites or applications. Completing your profile in its entirety demonstrates a conscientious approach to presenting yourself to others, consequently enhancing your likelihood of connecting with individuals who share similar preferences and interests.

Chapter 4

Be Honest with Yourself

We are instilled with the value of honesty from a young age. We receive instruction from our parental figures, as well as our elders and governing authorities, regarding the importance of practicing honesty in our interactions with both individuals and society. However, with what frequency do we deceive ourselves?

To what extent have you proclaimed verbally a statement that you hold no conviction in? On occasion, individuals resort to self-deception as a means to seek solace in the choices they are making or to secure victory in a debate with others. Nevertheless, deceiving oneself is a wholly inappropriate course of action.

Should one begin to engage in habitual self-deception, the inevitable consequence will be the fabrication of justifications and a gradual inclination towards a perpetually dissatisfied existence. The experience of fulfilling one's aspirations yields a significantly more contented existence compared to perpetually assuming the role of a victim.

Assume accountability for your choices, irrespective of their outcomes.

Furthermore, grant yourself the opportunity to alter your perspective. Exhibit a capacity for flexibility in light of life's circumstances. Individuals who possess an inherent obstinacy are prone to subjecting themselves to a perpetual existence of unhappiness rather than acknowledging an error or adjusting their perspective.

It commences with deceiving one's own self. It concludes with leading an existence devoid of purpose, characterized by the justification of one's own actions through the creation of excuses and the shifting of blame onto others. A significantly more favorable alternative is to sincerely assess oneself and subsequently pursue one's genuine aspirations.

Prior to delving into a discussion on honesty, it is imperative to contemplate the significance of one's image. What relevance does the concept of image hold in relation to honesty? Presenting oneself in a suitable manner goes beyond mere communication. It pertains to introspection and adherence to personal integrity.

Projecting the Right Image

Every action you undertake in life contributes to your overall "perception." Essentially, this pertains to the specific persona you desire others to perceive and associate with you. Regardless of your level of awareness, it is important to note that you are consistently projecting this "image" to the outside world.

Hence, if you genuinely intend to enhance your prospects in dating (or at the very least, garner more interest from individuals of higher quality for potential dates), dedicate efforts towards projecting a formidable image. I am not implying that you must present yourself with an outward appearance of success.

Perhaps the concept of adopting a pretense of achievement in order to encounter someone may appear insincere to you. I am not implying that you ought to feign anything. I am suggesting that you should consider giving more consideration to integrating your personality into your physical appearance.

In this manner, individuals will expeditiously ascertain your character. Fundamentally, you are instructing them on how to perceive you, rather than allowing them to develop a conventional classification. This approach not only serves as an efficient method to socialize, but also as a means to attract a suitable partner.

Consider the arduous task Mister Right faces when attempting to locate you amidst a vast pool of eligible individuals across the expanse of the United States. To identify your compatibility amidst a myriad of incompatible matches, he is compelled to meticulously sift through an assortment of unsuitable suitors, taking into account factors such as social standing, age, and geographical proximity. Consider the emotional impact he experiences as he diligently sifts through countless women who, regrettably, do not align with his preferences.

If he could only encounter an individual who possesses akin interests and lifestyle to his own. Indeed, discerning such information solely based on a basic headshot and a concise 140-word profile stating one's availability and interest in companionship might prove challenging. As such, what inclination does he tend to have initially? She seems...average. May I inquire as to the whereabouts of the image? Where does one find the manifestation of personality within an individual's physical presentation?

What Are The Defining Characteristics Of A Healthy Relationship?

Each relationship is unique, and there exist a multitude of factors that contribute to their formation. One of the hallmarks of a healthy relationship is the existence of a shared vision regarding the desired nature and future trajectory of the relationship. And the sole means to ascertain this is by engaging in an extensive and candid dialogue with your spouse.

Nevertheless, there are certain characteristics that the majority of healthy relationships have in common. A comprehensive grasp of these foundational principles can assist individuals in upholding a profound, fulfilling, and exhilarating bond, unaffected by any challenges or common objectives that may be in their collective endeavors.

You both still maintain a profound emotional bond. Each of you provides the other with a profound sense of affection and deep emotional satisfaction. The experience of receiving love and the sensation of being loved are separate concepts. When one experiences love, there is a sense of being valued and embraced by one's partner, as if there is a deep comprehension of one's being. Certain partnerships experience a sense of emotional detachment from each other, yet maintain a state of harmony. Despite the seemingly strong foundation of the relationship, the lack of sustained involvement and emotional connection only serves to further widen the rift between the individuals involved.

You are open to courteous disagreement. While certain couples may opt for private deliberation, others might engage in passionate disputes. Nevertheless, a key component of fostering a successful relationship entails embracing disagreements without trepidation. In order to maintain a secure environment for expressing concerns without the apprehension of repercussions, it is imperative that one possesses the capability to manage conflicts without employing derogatory strategies or an inflexible insistence on personal correctness.

You nurture your personal interests and connections beyond the realm of work. It is unrealistic to expect one individual to fulfill all of your desires, contrary to the depictions seen in romantic literature or films. Imposing unjustified expectations upon your partner has the potential to adversely impact a relationship. Nurturing your individual identity, cultivating your connections with loved ones, and fostering your personal pursuits will all contribute to invigorating and enhancing your romantic relationship.

You partake in sincere and transparent communication. Effective collaboration necessitates maintaining transparent channels of communication. Establishing mutual clarity and promoting open communication about desires, concerns, and aspirations could foster trust and strengthen the bond between both individuals.

Developing romantic feelings versus maintaining a committed relationship.

The majority of individuals hold the belief that the experience of falling in love is a spontaneous occurrence. Sustaining love or perpetuating the feeling of being in love necessitates a commitment and exertion of continual dedication. Considering the advantages, the effort is certainly justified. In times of prosperity and adversity alike, a robust and unwavering romantic bond has the potential to serve as a perpetual wellspring of delight and sustenance, enriching every dimension of your personal welfare. By exerting adequate efforts at present to sustain or reignite your initial experience of love, it is plausible to establish a enduring bond that endures for an extended period, potentially even a lifetime.

Numerous couples solely focus on nurturing their relationship when faced with specific, inescapable matters necessitating resolution. After the matters have been addressed, individuals often resume their professional responsibilities, familial commitments, or engage in other recreational pursuits. However, in order for love to flourish, romantic partnerships require unwavering attention and commitment. A romantic affiliation will necessitate your dedication and exertion as long as it retains significance to you. By acknowledging and resolving a minor issue within your relationship at present, you have the potential to prevent it from escalating into a more significant matter in the future.

You can sustain the experience of falling in love and cultivate a strong romantic partnership by employing the following guidance.

Recommendation 1: Allocate time for face-to-face interactions.
You develop feelings for one another by engaging in sustained eye contact and attentive listening. One might sustain the experience of falling in love over time if one consistently maintains an attentive demeanor, while actively observing and listening. It is undeniably true that you recall the commencement of your romantic union with your significant other with great affection. All facets appeared rejuvenated and captivating, undoubtedly prompting lengthy conversations or the conceiving of unique and captivating endeavors. Nevertheless, as time elapses, the burdens of work, familial obligations, various responsibilities, and the necessity for solitude on an individual level can impede our ability to allocate time for each other.

Numerous pairs observe that the rapid exchange of texts, emails, and instant messaging which once epitomized their initial courtship gradually supplant face-to-face engagements. Despite the numerous advantages of digital communication, it fails to yield the same positive impact on the cognitive faculties and neural pathways as in-person dialogue. Despite expressing feelings of love through digital or vocal communication, failing to regularly engage in direct, face-to-face interactions and dedicate time to one's spouse may lead them to believe that the sentiment is not fully comprehended or valued. Moreover, the bond between you and your partner will inevitably weaken or become more indifferent. Irrespective of the busyness of life, it is of utmost importance to allocate time for nurturing your relationship, as the emotional signals that both of you need to feel valued can only be conveyed in face-to-face interactions.

Devote to consistently allocating time for shared activities. Regardless of the level of busyness one may have, it is imperative to allocate a portion of each day dedicated to sincerely concentrating on and establishing a sincere connection with one's spouse. Please stow your electronic devices. Cease contemplating other matters. Discover a shared pursuit that appeals to both parties, whether it entails a pastime, participating in a dance class, taking regular leisurely walks, or simply indulging in a tranquil, morning coffee ritual.

Together, try something novel. An excellent strategy for fostering connections and maintaining novelty is to embark on novel endeavors as a collective unit. Embarking on a day trip to an unfamiliar destination or partaking in a dining experience at a novel restaurant are but a couple of straightforward instances. Aspire to derive amusement collectively. During the initial stages of a relationship, it is common for couples to exhibit elevated levels of enjoyment and vivacity. Nevertheless, in instances where challenges in life emerge or lingering resentments from the past intensify, it is possible for this lighthearted attitude to dissipate. Retaining a jovial demeanor can facilitate the management of challenging circumstances, alleviate stress, and foster resolution. Deliberate upon innovative approaches to astonish your significant other, such as spontaneously presenting them with a bouquet of flowers or securing a reservation at their favored dining establishment. Engaging in interactions with animals or young children may also aid in the restoration of one's innate sense of playfulness.

Dating an Athlete

An athlete is connected to sports, while the pursuit of physical fitness possesses an inherent capacity to reach particular physical objectives. Hence, a lifestyle as a professional athlete encompasses a range of responsibilities, including but not restricted to embarking on journeys and exerting maximum effort on the playing field, demonstrating exceptional physical prowess. Engaging in a romantic relationship with an athlete can offer an enjoyable experience, albeit one that requires adept handling of the highs and lows in order to foster the success of the partnership.

Engaging in relationships with athletes can offer romantic and thrilling experiences; however, sustaining such connections necessitates additional effort compared to other types of relationships, particularly if one desires a lasting commitment. This is due to the fact that athletes engage in activities that are not typical of other individuals. First and foremost, the individuals in question possess a significant abundance of female acquaintances who actively seek their attention from various regions of the nation, eagerly pursuing any opportunity to engage with them. Additionally, their itinerary is occupied with numerous commitments, which frequently entail extensive travel throughout the nation.

When they find themselves in a specific location during a certain period, it is either due to their presence at a training camp or engaged in interviews, consequently making them less accessible than one might assume.

It proves challenging to capture the focus of these individuals, as they contend with numerous diversions, and the majority exhibit limited urgency in terms of settling down expeditiously. However, it should be noted that there is no inherent detriment in pursuing romantic relationships with athletes. This is evident through the significant number of women who have successfully engaged and committed themselves to such individuals, even ultimately leading to marriage and the exchange of vows.

A significant number of individuals exert considerable effort to meet an athlete, as it is perceived as their conduit to a life of opulence. While they could be correct in their assessment, it is essential to acknowledge that achieving something worthwhile often involves considerable effort and challenges. Interacting with athletes can undoubtedly be enjoyable, yet it is imperative to acknowledge the presence of various obstacles. It is commonly held that engaging in a romantic relationship with an athlete is generally discouraged due to the perceived tendencies of inflated self-importance, limited dedication, and a propensity for promiscuity.

Please find presented below several factors to consider if you are engaging in a romantic relationship with athletes and desire to maintain a lasting connection.

1. Hectic agenda

Engaging in a romantic relationship with a professional athlete, whether they are present or available, poses considerable challenges. It is plausible that he might be present at a training facility or receiving guidance from a coach, or engaged in the process of interviewing individuals who are entering the profession. Dating an individual of this nature entails distinct circumstances compared to entering a romantic relationship with a colleague or individuals of a more conventional nature, predominantly due to their exceptionally busy and tightly scheduled lifestyle.

2. Grant them sufficient room

Professional athletes necessitate a conducive environment wherein they can carry out their responsibilities unhindered by any obtrusive elements that may interfere with their focus and concentration. Frequently, women tend to express dissatisfaction regarding the lack of attention they receive from their romantic partner, a desire which is typically sought after by all women during the process of dating. However, it is important to recognize that these women often have demanding professional commitments, and therefore may not react positively to individuals who intrude upon their personal boundaries and display excessive persistence.

The majority of gentlemen prefer to take the lead in pursuing their partner, rather than having her persistently pursue them. By allowing your date the space to contemplate your activities and generate curiosity about you, you can cultivate a sense of intrigue that instills a desire within him to learn more about you. Rather than relentlessly pursuing and constantly shadowing his every move, allow him the opportunity to pursue you.

3. Entice Him

A customary athlete experiences fatigue upon returning home as a result of the diligent efforts exerted throughout the day. Additionally, it is crucial to bear in mind that a majority of athletes experience fatigue throughout the course of a season in light of their professional commitments. Therefore work for it.

4. They possess financial stability.

One advantageous aspect of being in a relationship with an athlete is the diminished likelihood of encountering financial concerns, contingent upon the level of financial stability of your partner. Furthermore, in the event that he possesses substantial financial stability, it is probable that you will be afforded the privilege of residing in an exquisite abode and indulging in the luxury of owning high-quality automobiles.

5. Adopt proactive strategies.

Rather than becoming anxious about their activities during their absence, their frequency of seeking you out, or any irrational thoughts that could potentially lead to disagreements concerning their hectic schedule, it would be beneficial for you to immerse yourself in your own work and personal pursuits. It is crucial to embrace and cherish one's own existence even in the absence of the significant other, just as one would find joy in their presence.

However, the female athlete holds the belief in participating in a physically engaging outing. For the initial rendezvous, after obtaining her contact information in advance, it would be appropriate to send her a lighthearted electronic correspondence or engage in a whimsical telephonic conversation, in which you cordially invite her to part take in a miniature golf competition.

When she expresses her fondness for a physical activity that you have not yet experienced, such as yoga, propose that you are open to engaging in that activity alongside her, on the condition that she is also willing to reciprocate. During your subsequent encounter, it would be advisable for the two of you to engage in an activity of shared interest that is unfamiliar to her, such as visiting the batting cages or golf driving range.

Accompany her to participate in a tennis match, or any similar affable contention. In a short span of time, you will gain substantial insights into her personality and build a strong rapport with each other. Subsequently, engage in an enjoyable fitness session together, followed by the opportunity to have lunch together.

You may extend an invitation to her, proposing a visit to the park to engage in a recreational activity such as playing Frisbee or throwing a football. Bringing her to a public venue can significantly contribute to establishing a sense of security and trust between the two of you.

Additionally, the female athlete can readily become attracted to you, particularly if you already possess a keen inclination toward maintaining good health and physical fitness. Being highly dedicated to their physical fitness, athletes invariably find pleasure in frequenting the gym, willingly devoting a substantial portion of their day to workout sessions. Consequently, in order to maintain compatibility with your significant other, it may be necessary for you to also be present at the gym. You might enhance your physical condition by making the deliberate choice to invest effort in refining your physique.

If one finds pleasure in embarking on journeys, they will find great satisfaction in being involved romantically with an athlete, given their proclivity for frequent mobility. You have the potential to experience an upscale lodging experience with exceptional VIP amenities, which serves as the pinnacle of your overall experience.

Characteristics In Females Disliked By Males

When discussing characteristics disliked by males, I am referring to behaviors that elicit a strong aversion and diminish their interest. This does not pertain to inherent traits, such as height or skin color, which individuals cannot alter. These attributes refer to qualities that women employ in their endeavors to attract men. As previously stated in the introductory chapter, adopting a superficial persona in order to incite temporary attraction in a man is insufficient to sustain a lasting connection. In the event that any developments occur, you may potentially establish a companionship of mutual satisfaction, in which he maintains a relationship with an individual who possesses qualities of assurance, intellect, and spontaneity. The aspects in women that elicit disdain from men primarily pertain to our inclination towards engaging in seemingly insignificant behaviors, which stem from our misguided perception of fulfilling the expectations of men. Regardless of whether we have been instructed to behave in this manner or have adopted it based on past success, it is imperative that we now recognize these characteristics and permanently discard them.

Jealousy serves a purpose within the confines of a romantic partnership. Expressing dissatisfaction with your partner due to perceived instances of favoring another woman is a matter that can be addressed and resolved through open and constructive dialogue between the two of you as a committed couple. Upon initial acquaintance with an individual, should you experience a prompt, overwhelming sensation of jealousy due to the attention other females are bestowing upon him, it is highly likely that his inclination to distance himself from you will exceed your most vivid imagination. It could be perceived as endearing to assertively vie for the attention of someone with whom you have recently become acquainted, but from the perspective of the individual in question, such behavior may be interpreted as exhibiting dependency, clinginess, and a sense of urgency. There is a possibility that he may accompany you to your home later during the evening, but I assure you that it will not evolve into a lasting relationship. He might encounter rejection from other girls and is fully aware that he already has you secured through the behavior you showcased earlier in the evening.

Possessing independent thoughts is commendable; however, there is a widespread belief among women that acquiescing to a man's desires will positively influence his affections. Irrespective of his statements, you consistently demonstrate your willingness and preparedness to engage in the endeavor. In the event of his inclination towards staying at home to watch a ball game or attending a movie theater outing, your stance remains impartial and you are prepared to fulfill the task. In the event that he inquires about your preferred plans for this evening, your consistent response should be aligned with his preferences. This will become tiresome rapidly, as gentlemen desire to acquire a deeper understanding of your interests and partake in activities that bring you pleasure. This is the manner in which the relationship will flourish. He will inevitably grow weary of taking charge since this is a capability he possesses with virtually any woman. Cease behaving as the individual who is hesitant to cause any disturbance or discomfort to the male counterpart, simply by engaging in activities that deviate from the norm. Demonstrate to him your capacity for originality and enjoyment.

If you perceive the behavior of dependence as endearing, it is inevitable that your relationship with this individual will be terminated in the near future. Although a supportive partner will be there for you during difficult times, it becomes tiresome if every day is a struggle. Men are disinclined to continuously undertake the task of coming to the aid of the distressed avian creature. If you believe that consistently seeking emotional solace from your partner by discussing the recurrent challenges in your life, with the intention of enhancing his sense of masculinity, you are regrettably under a misconception. Men derive a sense of masculinity from actively aiding others and are sincerely motivated to alleviate your discomfort. In a robust relationship, the anguish affects the gentleman to the same extent as it affects you. However, should you frequently experience distress on a daily basis due to the belief that he must consistently undertake efforts to resolve matters, it is likely that he will seek out a partner who does not exhibit such constant dependence. Focus on cultivating enjoyable experiences with your partner instead of relying on their constant intervention, and you will witness an increased longevity in your relationships with men. Allow me to provide you with some recommendations regarding the appropriate sources to locate suitable male individuals.

5. Don\\\'t give up.

The principal factor contributing to the perceived ineffectiveness of the Law of Attraction is the tendency of individuals to prematurely relinquish their pursuits prior to attaining their desired objectives. It can be likened to ordering a delightful lunch, only to depart the restaurant before the meal is served. If you fail to maintain the pace of the order, you will forfeit it, as it is already in transit.

In matters pertaining to matters of the heart, individuals often experience disillusionment upon finding that their romantic encounters do not live up to their expectations, ultimately leading them to overlook the indications of an impending genuine affection. Individuals often relinquish their pursuits due to disillusionment or apprehension regarding the prospect of failure, without truly comprehending the opportunities they forego.

The essence of the Law of Attraction lies in the unwavering dedication one must maintain towards their aspirations until they materialize, ultimately leading to the discovery of their true life partner.

6. Do not fluctuate amidst adversities.

We dwell in a realm of considerable accommodation, wherein every conceivable aspiration may be achieved.

Indeterminacy presents itself as a significant hindrance towards the realization of our aspirations. We have a desire, but we hold reservations about its feasibility. In fact, it is doubt that serves as an impediment to its realization.

Acquiring knowledge yields a beneficial force that enhances attraction. The closure of said door is attributed to the presence of scepticism and pessimism, thus enabling the manifestation of negative energy. It is commonly perceived that when one is making progress in the process of attracting a life partner, there exists a certain sentiment that their ideal spouse is drawing near.

7. Enjoy the present moment to the fullest.

Do not postpone the commencement of your life until you encounter love.

If one possesses a sedentary lifestyle, it is plausible that individuals of similar inclination will be inclined to gravitate towards them due to shared characteristics and tendencies. If you desire companionship with an individual of an active disposition, a penchant for skiing, and an appreciation for literature, engage in pursuits such as engaging in physical activity, partaking in downhill skiing, and spending time within the confines of a well-stocked bookstore.

In order to pursue a most fulfilling life, one should not delay for the appearance of another person. Commence embracing a fulfilling existence in the present moment, and you shall promptly exude remarkable beauty, rendering it feasible for an individual of significance to discern your presence amidst a gathering.

8. Adjust to your future self

There exists a current "singular you" and a prospective future spouse or companion.

As the individual already committed within a relationship, you possess one of the most effective approaches to leverage the Law of Attraction in order to draw in your ideal partner.

It operates in the following manner: mentally form images of both your current self and the ideal version of yourself that you aim to cultivate for a prospective relationship. What makes you unique? After the connection has been established, what is your subsequent identity?

Perhaps you may express, "I experience a sense of tranquility, confidence, affection, and benevolence." Your response will act as a guiding path towards the personal growth you should strive for in the present moment.

Do not delay for the establishment of the connection; commence behaving in the manner befitting an individual already possessing these attributes. Organizing your wardrobe, decluttering a storage compartment, or refreshing the worn-out wallpaper are all illustrative actions to prepare your residence for the ideal marital partner.

Examine all the potential ways in which you might be prepared for the ideal companion and for your life to seamlessly align.

9. Organize your beliefs.

Evaluate your romantic notions and relinquish those that hinder your ability to attract, sustain, or derive satisfaction from your desired relationship: "I lack sufficient physical attractiveness," I stated. I am not earning a sufficient income, as all the desirable opportunities are already unavailable.

If a belief is not aligned with one's true desires, it is advisable to release it and cultivate beliefs that are, as the world has the tendency to manifest one's beliefs into reality. The cosmos reacts to the perception one holds of oneself; should one feel inadequate or undeserving, the cosmos will reflect such sentiments.

10. Cease your contemplation of the method and instead have faith in its outcome.

We reside within an awe-inspiring realm that possesses the capability to fulfill your desires through remarkable and improbable means. Excessive preoccupation with such matters may impede the efficacy of the Law of Attraction.

Your aim is to articulate your aspirations with clarity and optimism, and to diligently pursue their realization by employing the aforementioned strategies. Do not become overly preoccupied with the means, as it is not within your purview.

If your objective is to minimize the probability of impeding progress and introducing superfluous complications, consider the following. Alternatively, relinquish any preconceived notions about the course of events and allow the cosmic forces to unfold their enchantment.

This does not imply that you should stay indoors and engage in inactivity.

The distinction lies in the fact that you anticipate engaging in motivated action. The term "inspired action" refers to an impromptu compulsion to engage in an activity without a specific reason, such as visiting a coffee shop despite lacking thirst or acquiring fuel from the opposite side of the street.

It is imperative to attentively heed and effectively respond to your intuition, as the Law of Attraction establishes communication through this channel.

Remain receptive to all possibilities, as the vastness of the universe is capable of surprising us in unforeseen ways.

Heal Your Body

Directly following an assault, it is conceivable that you may experience a sense of detachment from your physical self, as though your essence is detached and observing the incident from an elevated position. In the immediate aftermath of my massage incident, I experienced a complete absence of physical discomfort during the initial days. I experienced a sensation akin to witnessing the narrative of my existence unfold on a cinematic display. All elements appeared incredibly surreal, invoking a sensation that I could effortlessly place my hand above a blazing flame with no perception of pain. This sense of disconnection from existence is frequently experienced by individuals enduring Post-Traumatic Stress Disorder (PTSD). I regard this time period as a divine form of analgesics following a significant surgical procedure. It affords you a brief respite prior to resuming one's daily routines. However, it is important not to be deceived by the notion that one can prolong their stay in this phase beyond a few days. It is your destiny to proceed and make progress in your life.

Furthermore, I harbored strong aversion towards my physical appearance. I had no desire to experience emotions, particularly sadness. I ceased desiring to possess beauty. I consumed the maximum amount that I was capable of ingesting. Once more, partaking in food consumption as a means to avoid appearing attractive and vulnerable to potential aggressors inadvertently hinders your pursuit of ultimate happiness. Moreover, it fails to deter assaults.

The commencement of healing is initiated by the physical form of the individual. Previously, I held the belief that engaging in physical exercise and maintaining a healthy diet were merely concerned with appearances, yet they serve as effective measures in mitigating depression and fostering a more positive outlook on life. If one fails to prioritize self-care, their well-being is likely to be compromised. I advise implementing the subsequent adjustments to your lifestyle in order to promote your psychological recuperation from the distress: engage in regular physical activity, consult with your medical professionals, adhere to a nutritious diet, ensure sufficient rest, and seek enjoyment in your pursuits.

Exercise Often
In addition to seeking the assistance of a therapist, engaging in physical activity is a vital step to undertake following an incident of attack. If you have recently encountered a distressing event, establishing a connection with your physical self may be the least desirable option given the accompanying pain. However, it is essential to recognize that fostering a state of mental well-being necessitates the upkeep of a sound physical condition. I strongly recommend enrolling in a self-defense course or considering participation in a yoga program. If you are not inclined towards socializing, consider utilizing an

exercise video as an alternative. Simply focus on being present in your physical state and endeavor to attain a state of relaxation. Physical activity is an excellent means of achieving that goal. Devote a total of ninety minutes per week, subject to approval from your healthcare practitioner.

Regardless of your lack of motivation, engage in physical activity regardless. Depression frequently diminishes one's vitality by eroding the enjoyment derived from ordinary, routine activities. Make a concerted effort to engage in physical activity, and as the release of endorphins (neurochemicals in your brain) accompanies the exercise, you will experience an alleviation of your depression as well. Please remain cognizant of any detrimental thoughts pertaining to physical activity, yet refrain from indulging in them. Instead, proceed to engage in exercise. Indeed, whenever you are experiencing distress, engage in physical activity, even if it entails simply playing music and indulging in a fifteen-minute dance session within the confines of your residence. Here is the information/proposition

Physical activity stimulates the secretion of neurotransmitters and endorphins, known as 'feel good' hormones, in the brain. This invariably enhances mood and acts as a countermeasure against the prevalent melancholic state frequently encountered by individuals with depression. Physical activity also has an impact on brain-derived neurotrophic factors, which play a crucial role in safeguarding neuronal cells against harm and facilitating the transmission of mood-related signals within the brain. Exercise also holds potential mental advantages, such as fostering self-assurance and encouraging the establishment of objectives and optimistic thoughts. As a result, individuals coping with depression may experience a greater sense of inner balance and renewed optimism towards their lives.

The sole precaution I would like to emphasize is to engage in activities with a partner during daylight hours for the sake of safety. When engaging in outdoor exercise, it is advisable to always have a companion. Refrain from subjecting yourself to potential danger by engaging in solo jogging activities in a poorly illuminated park during the late hours of the night. I express this sentiment due to the potential temptation that may arise for you to explore your limits for further offensive actions or to deny the occurrence of the initial assault.

See Your Medical Doctor
Arrange appointments with your healthcare providers. In the event of experiencing sexual abuse, your gynecologist is capable of providing medical interventions for sexually transmitted infections. A multitude of sexually transmitted infections exhibit no symptoms and, if left untreated, can result in the obstruction of your fallopian tubes. Obtain comprehensive fertility assessments to ensure the preservation of your reproductive

capabilities. While this endeavor may carry considerable emotional weight, it is imperative for the sake of your overall well-being in the long run.

A primary care physician, whether they be a general practitioner or internist, is capable of formulating a comprehensive healthcare strategy. You potentially have a preexisting medical condition that may impede the process of recovering from your trauma. In addition to providing guidance regarding an appropriate exercise and dietary regimen, your physician can also assist in identifying potential factors that may render you susceptible to depression or anxiety. Do you have a deficiency in iron, vitamin B-12, or vitamin D? Perhaps it would be advisable to consider receiving a vitamin injection or incorporating dietary supplements into your regimen. Do you suffer from a thyroid disorder, hormonal imbalance, or sleep apnea? Each of these circumstances has the potential to induce depressive symptoms. I have been medically diagnosed with sleep apnea and anemia.

Certain medical professionals may recommend the use of prescription medications to treat depression or aid sleep. If you hold reservations concerning the usage of sleep medication or antidepressant pills, it would be advisable to seek out a physician who possesses expertise in natural or homeopathic remedies.

Additionally, I would suggest discussing potential modifications to your lifestyle with your healthcare provider. Beverages such as coffee, tea, and alcohol have the potential to induce feelings of anxiety and depression. Consider endeavoring to abstain from [activity] for a duration of one month, and observe the resulting alterations in your sleep patterns and emotional states. During the initial days, it is possible to encounter withdrawal symptoms such as experiencing severe headaches. Your physician can provide guidance on navigating this procedure.

Please engage in a comprehensive discussion regarding these various options with your healthcare provider, and subsequently collaborate with them to establish a coherent plan for achieving optimal health. I employed psychotherapy in conjunction with modifications to my lifestyle, embracing physical exercise, adhering to a balanced diet, and ensuring an adequate amount of sleep, in order to alleviate the depressive symptoms stemming from the traumatic incident.

The Correlation Between Achieving Success And Its Impact On The Search For A Life Partner.

Attaining success significantly contributes to discovering one's perfect life partner. Success is accompanied by numerous advantageous elements. You experience enhanced happiness, improved well-being, and a heightened sense of self-satisfaction as a result of achieving milestones in your life. Exuding a sense of contentment and inner tranquility will radiate a captivating aura that will draw others toward it. Few things are as remarkable as witnessing an individual brimming with genuine happiness. Attaining success is not solely defined by amassing wealth and indulging in a lavish lifestyle. Furthermore, it encompasses finding contentment in one's present circumstances and attaining desired objectives. Additionally, it pertains to the ability to accomplish objectives and aspirations. Individuals possess varied aspirations and long-term objectives. Various factors contribute to the subjective experience of happiness in each person.

Should you achieve success in your endeavors, you shall undoubtedly exude an aura of triumph, creating an illusion of impeccable perfection in all aspects of your life. Despite its imperfections, you consistently demonstrate the ability to resolve any challenge that arises. Individuals who achieve success demonstrate a heightened capacity for cognitive thinking and intellectual prowess. Hence, their adeptness in problem-solving, decision-making, and navigating the complexities of their daily routines is significantly facilitated. According to certain individuals, it is advisable for an individual to dedicate the initial portion of their twenties towards cultivating their identity and achieving personal success, while reserving the latter part of this decade for pursuing romantic relationships. This approach may not be universally applicable, but it is often advantageous to achieve success prior to cultivating romantic relationships and establishing a permanent partnership.

Individuals who exhibit signs of despondency will not likely elicit interest or appeal. Envision observing an individual with a countenance displaying despondency. Additionally, you may experience feelings of sadness and melancholy. These sentiments have the potential to be transmitted to another individual, resulting in a diminished affection towards individuals lacking the ability to display a genuine smile. If one frequently adopts a slouched posture, demonstrates a lack of motivation, or neglects to display even the most basic acts of benevolence, it is evident that their capacity to attract others will be greatly diminished. Substitute your pessimistic dispositions with optimistic ones, and subsequently, you will have the capacity to alter any situation. Wearing a pleasant smile can significantly enhance your appearance and impart a corresponding sense of positive well-being.

Prioritizing self-care is also crucial in the pursuit of finding a compatible life partner. It is highly unlikely that any woman would desire to assume the role of a mother to their significant others. They already have their biological mothers fulfilling that role. Ensure your own well-being, cultivate self-reliance, and strive for a fulfilling existence. These are the factors that greatly appeal to women. If one has achieved substantial financial success, it is imperative to exercise caution when selecting a partner, as certain individuals may be drawn to one's wealth rather than one's overall qualities and character. Financial resources possess the capacity to exert a significant influence, necessitating careful consideration and prudent action.

It is advantageous to establish connections with a diverse range of individuals, including women, in order to broaden one's array of choices. A negative aspect of the situation is engaging in numerous relationships and providing each of those women with false hope. Your lack of certainty regarding your desires warrants caution in leading women to have expectations of you. Familiarize yourself with their personalities, engage in meaningful conversations, and devote time to interpersonal interactions. However, it is crucial to refrain from making commitments or offering assurances that you are unable to fulfill. It will ultimately return to haunt you, exacting the severest consequences upon your own self.

Please bear in mind that the majority of women are inclined to be captivated by articulate expressions. Exercise caution and discretion when making statements or commitments to them. It would be undesirable for one to be characterized as the individual who manipulates and toys with the emotions of women. It is important to maintain awareness that women engage in extensive conversations covering a wide range of topics, making it plausible for two women to potentially cross paths and discuss matters pertaining to you. Encourage them to focus on a constructive subject matter. Being recognized as an individual with a pattern of superficial romantic relationships will inevitably hinder the quest for genuine love, as one must contend with the burden of a tarnished reputation. Treat women with kindness and take the effort to acquaint yourself with them. There exists a distinction between demonstrating kindness and engaging in flirtatious behavior towards every woman one encounters. Additionally, it is important to note that strong relationships are often built upon a foundation of friendship, and there is inherent value in establishing meaningful connections with others. Develop a wide network of acquaintances and explore the opportunities that may arise from these connections.

This may not present a significant challenge for individuals who have achieved success, as they are often afforded numerous privileges and advantages in such circumstances. They possess a proficient understanding and application of the principles of the law of attraction. Hence, it is advantageous to achieve success in one's personal endeavors prior to embarking on the pursuit of a compatible life partner and establishing a committed partnership. Additionally, it is essential to possess personal stability, rather than solely professional stability. It is imperative to maintain a sense of self-satisfaction and cultivate unwavering self-confidence. Should you possess numerous personal challenges, you will inevitably jeopardize interpersonal connections and potentially accept unsuitable relationships due to your unrestrained self-doubt.

Prior to inviting another individual into your life, it is imperative that you ensure you possess a positive self-assessment and a healthy sense of self. In order to cultivate affection for another individual, it is imperative to first establish a sense of self-love within oneself. How can one fully appreciate the presence of others without first learning to appreciate moments of solitude? Strive for personal growth, and you will attract fortunate circumstances, including finding love. Additionally, it is highly appealing to witness an individual who possesses the ability to lead their life in accordance with their own desires. Certain individuals adhere to societal norms and conform to established regulations, whereas others embrace a more exuberant approach to existence. The primary objective is to achieve a state of contentment. Experiencing joy will elicit numerous positive outcomes, and the state of happiness will enable you to radiate positivity to others. They will unquestionably perceive it and become drawn to it. Success brings about happiness as it enables one to obtain both their essential necessities and desired luxuries in life. You find yourself in a favorable position, wherein you have the capability to ensure the well-being of your loved ones. Hence, it is imperative to cultivate a victorious mindset in the pursuit of discovering one's soulmate.

Inconstancy in behavior is a consistently exhibited reaction...

The response indicates a lack of seriousness on his part. He is not prepared to meet the expectations you have set forth; had he been, the level of consistency would be readily apparent. He would exert sincere endeavor in order to achieve concordance between his words and actions, thus enabling the seamless alignment of all circumstances. He is either engaging in recreational activities or there is an unresolved matter that he has failed to attend to, consequently leading to the significant perplexity he is causing. Regardless, it is not something you should consider.

As previously stated in Chapter 2, it is important to differentiate between an individual who exerts sincere effort but occasionally errs and an individual who consistently encounters difficulties. When occurrences become regularized, they assume problematic proportions. Is he endeavoring to gain your approval? How would you describe his verbal expressions, and are they consistent with his behaviors? Despite the fact that actions carry greater weight than words, it is plausible to experience a sense of perplexity in this particular situation. His actions may suggest a desire to integrate himself into your life or establish a romantic connection with you, whereas his verbal communication expresses a contradictory sentiment.

The actions and verbal expressions must be in harmony.

There exists a discrepancy when actions and verbal expressions are incongruent. In some instances, an untruth may be propagated, or a matter is not being appropriately addressed. It necessitates further investigation and ought to be diligently attended to. When he asserts that you are not his romantic partner, that he does not perceive you as his girlfriend, and that he has no desire for a committed relationship, only to immediately behave contradictory to your expectations, he will promptly remind you, "I explicitly stated my lack of interest in having a girlfriend."

It is of utmost importance that you prioritize addressing the issue promptly, as it may very well be attributable to a mere misconception or breakdown in communication. Likewise, I acknowledge that should you attempt to address the issue, he may evade it skillfully, shifting the narrative to focus on yourself, your perceived shortcomings, or your alleged missteps. Accuse him of an interrogation and exerting pressure, thereby trapping yourself and diverting attention from the fact that he still hasn't addressed your inquiry. He failed to furnish you with any responses; consequently, the problem persists unresolved.

Each indicator leads to a consistent deduction: he lacks seriousness. He is not adequately prepared for a sincere and committed relationship, thus there is no justification for continuing to invest in it.

The individual divinely appointed for your companionship is in pursuit of a life partner, not an object of amusement. He is not endeavoring to deceive or manipulate you in any manner. The gentleman, who is considered divinely sanctioned, desires to establish a collaborative effort with you. He has exerted tremendous effort to reach this milestone, and now he aspires to collaborate with you in achieving further accomplishments. He harbors no intention to engage in deceit, befuddle you, or incite havoc within the realm of your existence. He is solely interested in ensuring your sense of security in his presence.

In order to establish a sense of security, the individual who truly values your presence will provide responses to your inquiries. He aims to demonstrate to you his distinction from the rest of the males. He seeks to instill in you the belief that he possesses exceptional qualities and genuine intentions in his interactions with you.

It is imperative to bear in mind that adolescent males may bring tumult and uncertainty, while a mature individual who harbors genuine intentions aims to foster lucidity and serenity within the relationship. Create a placard stating: EXCLUSIVELY FOR ADULT MALES. MINORS AND AMUSEMENTS ARE DISALLOWED.

if necessary. You have the opportunity to acquire that t-shirt; in fact, it is readily available to you. If I happen to witness any of you wearing that, I will not initiate legal action against you.

MEN ONLY. NO BOYS. NO GAMES.

However, ensure that you adhere to it consistently.

Do not merely discuss it; instead, embody it. It is imperative to acknowledge that you necessitate an individual with a serious demeanor, coupled with an unwavering preparedness and enthusiasm to invest substantial effort on your behalf.

Please understand that we are indeed emphasizing the specific quality that you should observe in him, however, it is important to constantly be mindful of your own energy. When you confess or reveal the truth, he is compelled to do the same. If, in the event that he is unable to arrive promptly, he must make the necessary arrangements to return to his place of residence. It\\\'s that simple.

Please be advised that it is important to refrain from engaging in emotional manipulation. Do not trifle with a gentleman's emotions unless you desire him to reciprocate.

Online Dating And Communication

Effective communication and the realm of online dating are intricately intertwined. Given the initial constraints on direct communication between you and your potential future partner, it becomes imperative to gain proficiency in effectively engaging with the available limited channels of communication. This section will comprehensively address the appropriate timing of communication, the allocation of financial responsibilities for online interaction, and the suitable content deserving of expression once the relationship commences.

Remit payment in order to correspond or exercise patience until a response is received?

If you are a male individual striving to cultivate an honorable and chivalrous impression, it is advisable not to rely on the female counterpart to initiate conversation by virtue of their financial contribution. It does not pertain to financial capacity; rather, it pertains to a commendable display of courtesy. It is incumbent upon the male individual to demonstrate sincere interest in the female counterpart by displaying a level of commitment and willingness to invest in the relationship.

The rate at which a relationship develops greatly relies on the regularity of communication. Please bear in mind that "communication" should not be viewed as a unilateral endeavor, but rather as a reciprocal interaction involving the exchange of ideas and information pertaining to one another. The realm of online dating boasts a vast user base comprising millions of individuals, inevitably leading to situations where a woman may find herself faced with the decision of selecting between two distinct suitors. Do you perceive that she will opt for the individual who compels her to incur expenses solely to maintain open channels of communication?

During the initial phases of engaging in online dating, it is commonly acknowledged that the level of expenditure is typically regarded as being directly correlated with one's level of interest. This assertion equally pertains to women. If a lady chooses to expend resources in order to reciprocate a gentleman's advances, affirming his interest in her, it indicates her genuine attraction towards him. It is recommended to exercise caution and refrain from providing an immediate response. Allow a few days to elapse before you provide a response to someone's electronic mail. By adopting this approach, you can avoid coming across as overly eager and maintain an air of intrigue.

What is the Appropriate Duration for Online Communication Prior to Advancing?

The latest surveys indicate that a majority of individuals do not perceive the allure of protracting the initial rendezvous. Several individuals expressed that a protracted period of waiting ultimately resulted in missed chances to secure a romantic encounter.

The individual under their consideration encountered an alternative individual to engage with, and the interaction between them transpired satisfactorily.

Online dating is primarily employed by individuals seeking efficient means to locate a prospective romantic partner, in contrast to the traditional methods of dating. Online users do not exhibit impatience or desperation, rather, they hold a significant regard for in-person interactions. If there is a strong dynamic between the two of you in your online interactions, and the person in question demonstrates themselves to be reliable and dependable, it may be worth considering pursuing a relationship.

It is purported that individuals refrain from prolonging online communication beyond a span of 14 days prior to arranging an in-person meeting for the purpose of a date. This time frame provides a practical opportunity for both parties to gain sufficient understanding of one another. During the initial encounter, individuals may choose to further explore and appreciate each other's attributes, thereby deepening their understanding and connection.

Guidelines for Effective Online Chatting

Frequently, individuals abuse online chatting as they allow their egos and emotions to dictate their words. The absence of effective communication skills will undoubtedly manifest in the manner in which an individual interacts with others in online conversations, and individuals who lack spontaneity are seldom afforded another opportunity. Hence, it is recommended to actively participate in the discourse.

When conversing with a prospective partner online, it is important for men to bear in mind three essential aspects: communicate with utmost courtesy, provide meaningful responses, and endeavor to empathize with her perspective. The initial principle asserts that all your messages should exhibit respect. Please refrain from discussing topics related to sex or anything of a similar nature that may cause her discomfort. Furthermore, it is imperative that her words are not disregarded. Indeed, individuals can still exhibit poor listening skills while interacting through online platforms; therefore, it is important to attentively listen and provide appropriate responses.

Women also tend to be attracted to men who possess insightful ideas and engage in meaningful conversations. Engaging in discussions about mundane subjects such as the weather will not contribute to gaining her attention. It is imperative to showcase your intellectual prowess while maintaining a respectful demeanor in order to capture her interest. Intellectually astute and polite gentlemen are easily captivating. One can also enhance their intellectual image by adopting the perspective of the individual in question. Women appreciate it when men demonstrate comprehension of their experiences. They desire men who possess a capacity for empathy.

For women, display an appreciative demeanor towards his humor and question his notions in a thought-provoking manner. Indeed, it is true that males have a propensity towards visual stimulation, nevertheless they exhibit endurance and commitment towards women who possess depth and substance, rather than mere physical attractiveness. Engage in intellectual discourse with him, and in moments when he approaches you online soliciting guidance on how to capture your affection, your response should not provide a straightforward resolution, but rather compel him to ponder further. Your replies are expected to be concise, captivating, and subtly enigmatic in nature. Typically, males have a tendency to be less inclined toward reading lengthy messages; hence, they are likely to value your endeavors in maintaining concise yet captivating content.

When to Engage in Telephonic Communication

This is largely contingent upon individual circumstances, as the progression of each relationship exhibits considerable diversity. A colleague's internet-based relationship may be progressing at a quicker rate compared to yours, as they have already commenced engaging in verbal communication through phone conversations. Nevertheless, do not succumb to the pressure. Rather, evaluate your existing communication infrastructure.

Are you sufficiently at ease during your conversations with him or her to confidently determine that it is now appropriate to engage in vocal communication? It is indeed more effortless to gain knowledge about an individual through phone communication, as compared to the impersonal medium of email. By means of the phone, one can perceive the individual's responses, the timbre of their speech, and the endearing nature of their laughter.

It is widely believed that engaging in successful email correspondence for a few weeks is typically adequate before progressing to communication via telephone. The relationship will either progress or terminate once communication is established between both individuals via telephone. Another benefit of this is that it facilitates seamless communication, enabling individuals to easily reach out to one another and inquire about their well-being throughout the day. An internet connection is unnecessary to gather information about the individual you are contemplating going on a date with.

Certainly, in the standard progression of online dating, it is customary to proceed from an initial kiss towards engaging in general email exchanges, participating in a series of chat sessions through the online chatting platform, and subsequently transitioning to a few phone conversations. The duration of this period can vary from one week to two weeks, contingent upon the frequency of communication and the level of connection that you experience between yourselves. Engaging in online conversations may bring a sense of excitement, yet conversing through the telephone indisputably offers an authentic sense of the individual you are preparing to encounter. It is recommended to engage in several telephone discussions prior to the scheduled meeting. You may utilize the telephone conversations as a platform to engage in discussions regarding cultural disparities, mutual relationship expectations, and anticipated interactions upon future encounters. Frequently, women may experience uncertainty regarding the anticipated outcomes and expectations upon meeting. Engaging in a telephone conversation can facilitate the establishment of these expectations, thereby alleviating any ambiguity.

You transform into an individual who effectively channels emotional intensity

The cultivation of concentration, when allotted sufficient duration, engenders a state of emotional imperative. Merely directing singular attention to a matter at a given moment will yield minimal results. While it possesses the ability to elucidate matters, there appears to be a discernible absence. It is imperative to possess a strong awareness of emotional urgency. It is imperative for you to understand that the present moment is the opportune time to initiate action. In the absence of such a sense of urgency, one's level of motivation to undertake action tends to be insufficient. In a similar vein, your energy level is insufficient to consistently take action on a daily basis.

I have some information to share with you. It is important to note that merely taking action does not guarantee success. That is not how it functions. Merely attempting a shot at the rim does not guarantee that the ball will successfully make it in. Consistently carrying out actions is imperative for achieving maximum success. It also requires resiliency. Undeniably, in a majority of instances, when embarking on a course of action, it is highly probable that failure will be the outcome. It doesn't pan out.

Upon thoroughly perusing the contents of this book, you are encouraged to deliberate upon implementing the prescribed steps therein. Subsequently, venture forth with the intention of acquainting yourself with novel female acquaintances. It is likely that initially, there will be limited success in the first attempts. It is imperative to possess a profound emotional impetus in order to consistently persevere and make attempts repeatedly. Experiment and combine various elements until a viable solution is achieved. This trait is commonly referred to as resilience, which necessitates harnessing the strength derived from possessing a sense of emotional urgency.

The principle of the law of attraction facilitates personal transformation, elevating one's emotional intensity to a heightened level. You would have a heightened capacity to endure additional challenges and adversities compared to previous circumstances. You would possess the capacity to confront your fears head-on and make a conscious decision to not succumb to their influence as significantly as previously.

Take action

You undergo a transformation when you initiate alternative courses of action. Engaging in activity alone will not inherently alter the course of your life, as pursuing the incorrect actions can ultimately lead to stagnation or regression. Indeed, it is possible that you may find yourself in a more unfavorable situation. In order to achieve optimal results, it is essential to execute appropriate actions, predicated upon discerning and articulating precise thoughts. Ensuring unwavering concentration on pertinent matters is imperative, facilitating an unobstructed focus. Such dedication should transpire alongside a deep-seated sense of emotional urgency.

Fortunately, when decisive measures are pursued, the global community takes notice and gives due regard. This is the point at which things assume an objective nature. This is the juncture where individuals commence to approach matters with earnestness. You are free to engage in conversation to your heart's content. You possess the ability to articulate persuasively; however, ultimately, your actions determine the true outcome. How do you behave? How do you act? What types of alterations do you bring about in your vicinity? This necessitates a transformation in your character, as it is evident that maintaining your current self would yield analogous outcomes that are predictable and familiar.

Furthermore, the process of taking action entails consistently and progressively amplifying one's efforts. Many individuals lack comprehension in this matter. They think that, "OK. "I will utilize the principle of the law of attraction along with harnessing the strength of vivid mental imagery in order to initiate and harmonize various contributing factors, subsequently leading me to initiate action." They subsequently conclude their statement. No, that is not the correct procedure. It is imperative that you persist in taking proactive measures, with a particular emphasis on expanding your operations. It is imperative that you expand your repertoire of actions. You must broaden your spectrum of intensity and expand your repertoire of actions. It is imperative that you consistently maintain focus on the mental representation and concept that you envision, persevering until your desired outcome is achieved.

Ultimately, the conclusion is that one emerges from the process transformed, indicating a successful execution; otherwise, it could be inferred that the process was not carried out effectively. If the law of attraction is diligently applied, it is inevitable that one will experience transformation. One inevitably experiences personal growth. The final outcome is uncomplicated.

The power of one's intentions materializes into a novel realm of existence. If one were to attend closely to the aforementioned Confucius quote, it becomes evident that by cultivating suitable thoughts, an individual can transform into a morally upright individual. It revolves around attaining the desired outcomes, and achieving them necessitates initiating the process with proper contemplation. This does not pertain to an instance where an individual simply shuts their eyes and engages in a cognitive exercise of envisioning these captivating visuals. You are simply indulging in optimistic speculation at that juncture. Merely having hope will not bring about any changes for you. It is imperative to allow the entire procedure to unfold.

The significance of having lucid ideas is paramount, yet it is imperative to couple them with thorough introspection and analysis of oneself. This process facilitates concentration, fostering a profound emotional drive that ultimately translates into proactive measures. After initiating a course of action, you are obliged to see it through without abandon. You must persevere in taking decisive measures and enhance the scope of your endeavors. This distinction lies between the realms of hoping, wishing, and the actualization of a triumphant existence. Which of these would you prefer to obtain?

Engaging & Investing

In the preceding chapter, I provided a concise discussion on fostering an authentic and exemplary demeanor in the presence of your romantic partner. To all individuals endeavoring to locate companions or partners, it is essential not to assume an altered persona that veers from your authentic self. Not only will you experience discomfort as you deepen your acquaintance with the individual, but you will also ultimately engage in self-deception. It is crucial that you maintain honesty with yourself.

When one is at ease with oneself, there is a higher probability of being able to unwind in the presence of gatherings. The consideration of potential judgment from others will hold no significance for you as your primary focus lies on engaging with unfamiliar individuals. There is also the possibility that you could exert influence over other individuals. You will act without being burdened by others' opinions and prioritize your own needs and desires. This mindset does not stem from self-centeredness, but rather indicates a strong sense of self-assurance.

Therefore, it is pivotal that you actively interact with and wholeheartedly commit to fostering your relationship once you have established a sense of ease with the other person.

Several methods to accomplish this objective include:

1) The ability to listen attentively confers a substantial advantage. This demonstrates your appreciation for your partner's words and conveys a genuine sense of concern. A proficient listener would pose thought-provoking inquiries, whereas an individual simply occupying time would demonstrate a lack of attentiveness to even the slightest particulars. An attentive individual would exhibit more receptive nonverbal cues, whereas an indifferent person would not even direct their gaze

towards the speaker. Frequently, individuals are capable of discerning whether or not you are actively engaged in listening, and this ability has the potential to enhance or undermine the quality of a relationship.

2) An additional course of action you might consider is actively participating in their discourse through the formulation of thought-provoking inquiries. One should refrain from making judgments about their narratives, as such evaluations can deter the individuals from sharing further experiences. This is due to the potential for them to feel misunderstood and develop a sense of mistrust. Do not inquire about matters that solely serve your own interests, but rather pose questions that will stimulate their thinking. Empathize with their perspective when they share details about themselves, and react correspondingly.

3) Upon thoroughly addressing the inquiries that emerged as a result of

attentively hearing out your significant other, it is likely that they will reciprocate by posing a question pertaining to yourself. Engage in honest and transparent communication, inject humor into your interactions, and refuse to confine your emotions. This will facilitate the exposure of your vulnerable aspect to your partner, thereby fostering a more resilient bond between the both of you.

4) Disseminate the aspects that bring you joy to your acquaintances and embrace the things that hold significance to your cherished companion. While it is crucial for both of you to avoid despising everything that you individually cherish, it is highly likely that you will not always share the same affection for each other's preferences. Therefore, it is essential that you acknowledge and wholeheartedly accept this reality, while also embracing one another despite these minor differences.

5) Whether it is in the serene ambiance of a nocturnal park, enjoying a refined concoction of Pina Coladas, or engaging in a playful game of tug of war with a beach ball in a tranquil swimming pool, partaking in meaningful moments will give rise to treasured reminiscences and cultivate a profound connection between yourself and your significant other.

Once you have encountered someone who appreciates your sense of humor and puts you at ease, take the time to discern the aspects that genuinely resonate with you and ascertain the compatibility between yourself and this individual. Reflect upon whether your appreciation for them is solely derived from their ability to evoke laughter or is it derived from their ability to elicit laughter from you specifically in times of stress awareness. Consider evaluating whether you experience a positive atmosphere in their presence and if your respective strengths and weaknesses align effectively. Inquire whether all three pins of the triangle are present, and if not, ascertain the feasibility of constructing the missing pin or pins. These are decisions that must be considered when seeking a person who will truly value your authentic self and provide support. Furthermore, these decisions will also determine if the connection with this partner can be defined as love. Should it not meet this criterion, you will be compelled to make determinations regarding subsequent courses of action.

The Emerging Frontier Of Online Dating

You are the epitome of deserving love and affection, surpassing all others in the vast expanse of the universe.

During this unparalleled era, we have been provided with the chance to halt, contemplate, and direct our attention towards the aspects that hold genuine significance in our lives. Remarkably, the inclination for social distancing has supplied numerous individuals with essential personal limits.

I was raised during an era in which children were expected to be seen but not heard, and there was a lack of emphasis on instilling the notion of establishing personal boundaries. We lacked privacy, and there was a general lack of appreciation for the significance of solitude. This situation evokes a reminiscent image from a Woody Allen film, where the spouse finds themselves confined within the bathroom while being subjected to their partner's impassioned verbal outpourings from beyond the impenetrable door. My mother took the initiative to answer the phone call and often attentively monitored the conversation on the other line until I respectfully requested for her to disconnect the call.

As I have matured, I have come to understand the significance of cultivating autonomous relationships that entail robust boundaries. In my fifties, a significant shift occurred where I found myself lacking the vitality or inclination to invest in unfavorable circumstances.

I experienced certain health issues last year, which I came to understand were the consequence of my involvement in circumstances characterized by inadequate boundaries.

The stress I experienced had a detrimental impact on my immune system, rendering me more vulnerable to illnesses. I hereby affirm that I shall cease to compromise my well-being amidst circumstances that could pose significant danger.

In order to experience healing and personal growth, it is imperative that we collectively confront our innermost selves, as Carl Jung famously articulated, and engage in introspective endeavors at some juncture in our lifetime.

For individuals to cultivate wholesome and enriching relationships, it has dawned upon me that both parties must engage in introspection and acknowledge detrimental behaviours, thereby facilitating personal growth and positive change.

This interval has provided me with the opportunity to reassess my individual limits and develop a renewed recognition of their significance and the liberty they afford. Limits enable us to establish effective communication with others, clearly indicating what is acceptable and what is not, while simultaneously safeguarding our personal space and preserving our energy.

Personal boundaries encompass physical, emotional, spiritual, or relational limitations aimed at maintaining a respectful distance from others. Instead of assimilating others' beliefs, standards, and emotions, establishing boundaries involves cultivating self-awareness regarding our own convictions, principles, and emotional responses. We acquire the capacity to cultivate a more robust and individuated identity, enabling us to exercise agency over our priorities and make choices that align with our established principles."

Remarkably, if one has previously encountered difficulties establishing boundaries with family members, it is highly probable that similar challenges will manifest within their personal relationships.

Needy, co-dependent relationships lack proper establishment of healthy boundaries, exemplifying the absence thereof. The removal of personal boundaries compels individuals to forsake their own sense of self, as they strive to acquire outward love and affection by fulfilling the needs and expectations of those around them. When individuals relinquish their personal identity in order to conform to external expectations, they experience a dilution of their selfhood and a depletion of their self-worth.

Certain individuals hold others accountable for their emotions and subsequent behaviors, thereby positioning themselves as the aggrieved party.
They anxiously await the intervention of someone to provide them with the affection and care that they profoundly

desire. They have relinquished all authority in the proceeding.

Establishing and maintaining healthy boundaries grants individuals the opportunity to strengthen their personal agency and, ideally, imparts to those around them the value of doing so as well. Please keep in mind that assuming that responsibility on their behalf is not incumbent upon you. Developing self-compassion is the fundamental element of this undertaking.

If one were to find themselves in such a situation, it is advisable to contemplate whether they are providing assistance or facilitating.

The act of enabling is frequently camouflaged as support, however, consistently absolving an individual from the repercussions of their own actions perpetuates patterns of unhealthy behavior.
Establishing proper boundaries can potentially prompt individuals in your

social sphere to assume accountability for their respective troubles and concerns.

By refraining from constantly intervening and rescuing them, you empower individuals to tap into their innate capabilities, thereby facilitating the realization of their utmost potential. Alternatively, if they do not address this issue, they will persist in seeking answers and solutions externally, resulting in a sense of dependency, inadequacy, and powerlessness.

8) You still have lingering unresolved matters stemming from your early years. Alternative way: Numerous households and family units in the world exhibit dysfunction, encompassing children affected by divorce or parental conflicts that persistently arise.
As our cognitive development may have been irrevocably influenced by the adverse and aggressive encounters we encounter during childhood.

We tend to exhibit similar behavioral patterns towards our partners as those ingrained in us during childhood, despite perceiving ourselves as emotionally well-adjusted and mature individuals.

Given our upbringing's ingrained perception of enduring partnerships and our limited knowledge on alternative perspectives.

How to discover a romantic connection: If you identify with this situation, it is not advisable to continue dating in the hope of finding an individual who can 'cope with' or accommodate your personality.

Upon encountering an individual who embodies kindness and selflessness, inevitably you will find yourself entangled within a detrimental and dysfunctional partnership with that individual.

The resolution lies in confronting your challenges and assuming personal responsibility for their resolution.

Comprehend the past instances of childhood trauma that are manifesting as detrimental behaviors, and undertake all measures essential to assimilate and process them within oneself.

9) You experience a profound sense of deserving unconditional love.

Incorrect approach: placing trust in the depictions portrayed in films and the enchanting stories that romanticize the concept of love as being unwavering and unconditional.

If an individual truly harbors affection towards you, they will remain steadfastly by your side during both the prosperous and challenging moments. Regardless of any adversities you may confront together, they will consistently offer unwavering support and remain a reliable presence in your life.

Appropriate alternative: The term "unconditional" does not truly signify "irrevocable."

Unwavering love does not imply that your partner must continue to love you despite your egregious actions, such as subjecting them to abuse (whether emotional or physical), disregarding their worth, or consistently criticizing them.

If you seek an individual who will offer unwavering affection towards you, it may require a substantial duration to find someone who will love you unconditionally.

When the affection between them begins to diminish, it is important not to perceive their actions as a letdown or betrayal, as it may simply indicate their inability to cope during your most challenging moments. Rather, you must display a willingness to put in the effort.

10) You overdo it.

Incorrect approach: We acknowledge your inclination for love above all else.

The sensation of advancing in age instills a genuine desire to embark on the noble pursuit of starting a family with a suitable partner, while well-meaning loved ones diligently encourage you to pursue romantic endeavors.

Upon the commencement of a date, one may perceive the imminent resonance of wedding bells.

Even if you refrain from expressing your level of desperation, it is readily detectable to others, even from a significant distance away. One could argue that there are few characteristics that are as unappealing as displaying a sense of desperation.

The correct approach entails simply engaging in relaxation and adopting a laid-back disposition.

Whilst it is indeed possible to encounter an ideal companion and aspire to establish a lasting relationship with them, it is imperative to acknowledge that the realm of dating can be likened to a strategic pursuit. In this endeavor, practitioners must exercise prudence, ensuring that an excessive longing for companionship does not impede their ability to conduct comprehensive assessments of potential partners.

The act of appearing excessively assertive or forward in a premature manner may elicit an uncomfortable reaction from individuals. You must establish the perception that you possess enduring qualities that make you a highly desirable individual.

The Wedding Day

The commencement of our wedding day mirrored countless others, characterized by its sheer beauty and a pervasive sense of optimism. I was filled with joy as I contemplated an eternity together with the person whom I adore immensely. Notwithstanding, a sense of unease was detectable. Throughout the entirety of the morning, I experienced a sense of unease and apprehension. Upon further reflection, I came to the realization regarding the reason behind it: the moment had arrived for our inaugural dance. As we gently moved in synchronization with the melodic cadence of our chosen composition, I fixed my gaze upon his eyes. Anticipating a warm and affectionate response, I was surprised to find his countenance transformed by intense fury. I succeeded in maintaining a congenial countenance while inquiring about his abrupt decline in enthusiasm.

He quietly expressed his grievances concerning my family's perceived disrespect towards his closest companion, resulting in his decision to abstain from participating in the dance. I was astonished!

"So, you prioritize your best friend over me and our first dance?" I retorted, making an effort to remain composed.

In a state of displeasure, he casually dismissed the matter without delay. "Yeah."

At this juncture, I could no longer feign a smile, causing my countenance to redden with a blend of shame and fury. This was the day of my wedding, a day that every young woman envisions with hope and excitement. Yet, despite its significance, my husband treated me with indifference, as if I were an insignificant and neglected possession. It was at that juncture when I realized the error of my decision. The surrounding space began to constrict around me, inducing lightheadedness. I was uncertain whether to express my astonishment vocally, shed tears, retreat from the dance floor abruptly, or perform all of those actions simultaneously. I found myself hesitant to remain and hesitant to depart, as a multitude of individuals observed our presence, the optimism enveloping their spirits, and their felicity radiating towards us.

Regrettably, by that point, we had already entered into matrimony. So, I stayed. I suppressed my anger and remained reticent for the rest of the evening.

Subsequent to the wedding ceremony, my spouse administered disciplinary actions towards me owing to his sense of discontentment. He rescinded our planned honeymoon and completely disregarded any form of communication with me for a duration of seven days. The night of my wedding was unequivocally the most dreadful night I have ever experienced. Tears cascaded down my face as I reclined beside him, night after night, his back invariably facing me. This marked the inception of my new existence, which I harbored immense disdain for. As time went by, his level of control and emotional abuse escalated. He punished me often.

He roused from slumber one evening, abruptly inquiring, "Are you engaging in infidelity with another?"

"Absolutely not!" I replied in a state of disbelief.

He proceeded at length, stating, "I had a dream in which you were involved, therefore it must be true."

Subsequently, he abstained from engaging in conversation with me for a duration of two weeks and consistently undermined my person during opportune moments. Expressions such as "your physical strength is lacking," "your intellectual capabilities are insufficient to embark on an entrepreneurial venture," or "in the event of our dissolution, your prospects of attracting a suitable partner would become limited" were commonly used. The onslaught of his insecurities devastated his creative faculties, leaving me vulnerable to the merciless gales it wrought. Each strike inflicted upon me fractured my confidence into innumerable fragments. I made a conscious effort to abstain from indulging in his tirades, consistently reinforcing my affection towards him and affirming my commitment to his well-being. However, despite the torrent of sorrow that cascaded down my cheeks, it failed to satiate his insatiable desire for dominance. Our communication was minimal, and this persisted for a number of weeks. He went so far as to decline accommodations in the same bed, utilize the same bathroom, or coexist in any shared areas with me.

I experienced a greater sense of isolation within the confines of matrimony compared to the period of my singleness. What actions had I taken that were deemed as highly reprehensible? I cherished him with every fiber of my being. What was the cause of his lack of reciprocation towards me? What could have been the cause of his animosity towards me? I desired to bare my soul and demonstrate to him the genuine depth of my affection. I desired to alleviate the suffering that burdened him, prompting his outbursts, yet his heart seemed distant, gradually straying beyond reach.

I had ultimately developed a deep affection, only to find that my feelings were not reciprocated. Why Lord?

It was a weight that I deemed insufferable—an overwhelming, stifling ordeal.

My family and friends attributed it to typical challenges experienced in a marriage and provided reassurances that the situation would improve. So, I stayed. I was previously among the group of women who vocally expressed their determination to never tolerate any form of mistreatment from men. Additionally, I held the belief that a woman who endured abuse was simply lacking judgement in choosing to remain in such a situation. And here I am now, placed in a situation which I had vehemently vowed would never manifest in my existence.

One aspect that had eluded my awareness was the gradual onset of an abusive relationship, wherein one becomes acclimated to its harmful effects even before realizing its grip.

I harbored immense fear in severing ties with him due to the deeply ingrained values of my religious beliefs and my adherence to Nigerian cultural norms, both of which strictly disallowed divorce as a conceivable recourse. As an African wife, it is expected that you persevere, demonstrate resilience, engage in prayer, and show reverence towards your husband. I sought to uphold the dignity of my family, and moreover, I aimed to evade the arduous ordeal of recommencing the intricate process of courtship and matrimony. In light of everything, acquiring affection proved to be no small feat. So, I stayed. The more I prolonged my presence in an attempt to demonstrate my affection and pacify his indignation, the more I sacrificed my own sense of identity. His words commenced to taint my mind, instilling within it the pernicious notions he articulated concerning my persona, thus leading me to internalize them. Attempting to resuscitate him resulted in the gradual demise of various aspects of my being: my elation, my optimism, my self-assurance, my belief. I discontinued my participation in church volunteering, ceased socializing with friends, and refrained from visiting family members. I exhibited unwavering commitment towards enhancing his abilities, even as I endured personal deterioration. He assumed a deity-like status in my life, and the absence of such an authentic divinity results in the forfeiture of the fundamental essence of one's existence.

It could be contended by many that emotional abuse poses a significantly lesser risk compared to physical abuse. Nevertheless, I would like to present an alternative perspective by rephrasing this well-known proverb: "While physical harm may cause one's bones to fracture, it is crucial to acknowledge that verbal expressions possess the capacity to profoundly shatter one's inner being."

Words and detrimental actions possess the ability to inflict emotional wounds that are considerably more enduring and challenging to recover from. This is due to the fact that spirit fractures necessitate intervention from the curative influence of the divine. It is a protracted and uncomfortable procedure. Do not entertain the misconception that the absence of physical harm negates the possibility of being trapped in an abusive relationship. I certainly found myself in a state of distress, and my morale was deteriorating.

1. Ascertain the ability to perceive when the relationship manifests a seamless quality for all parties involved.

Occasionally, it is mentioned that an ideal relationship is characterized by its perceived simplicity. Nevertheless, it is pertinent to acknowledge that even the most excellent connections necessitate substantial effort and can be challenging occasionally. Regardless, it is frequently emphasized that a satisfactory relationship is characterized by a sense of effortlessness. It is not due to the absence of effort, but rather because both partners contribute and dedicate time, rather than one individual single-handedly shouldering the entire workload of the relationship. The pursuit of romantic relationships involves as much introspection as it does engagement in various activities.

2. Correspond to his level of commitment.

In the event that you are ultimately dismissed, provide him with an equivalent compensation in return. You may inherently feel inclined to establish a connection and promptly ascertain the situation. It may seem paradoxical to your current emotional state, but instead of resorting to phone communication to message him, I suggest you continue living your life. The pursuit of romantic relationships should not take precedence over other aspects of your life. Refrain from accessing online entertainment and cease obsessing over whether you might or might not be responsible for this; it is unrelated to you. If someone does not exhibit strong enthusiasm towards you, then their lack of interest is significant. In my perspective, conflicting signals are non-existent; he is either genuinely interested or he is not.

3. The Epitome of Dating/Relationships Wisdom on the Internet - Generously Supported

If you possess comprehension of this matter, I strongly recommend considering Relationship Hero, a distinguished online platform offering the services of highly skilled relationship coaches. These experts possess the ability to grasp the intricacies of your situation and provide invaluable guidance, aiding you in successfully attaining your desired outcome. They provide guidance and support in navigating intricate and challenging romantic situations, including deciphering conflicting signals, moving forward after a breakup, or any other concerns that may be causing you distress. You promptly establish a connection with an exceptional mentor through a written correspondence or by means of a telephonic conversation within a matter of minutes. Simply click here...

4. Establish the points of cessation from the commencement.
Boundaries play a crucial role in interpersonal relationships, as they symbolize individual preferences and expectations regarding personal treatment by others. Undoubtedly, prior to surpassing any boundary, it is imperative to engage in a discussion regarding what you are willing to tolerate and what you are not. This also aids in demonstrating to others the manner in which one should be treated. Frequently, when seeking their approval and desiring affection, establishing boundaries within the realm of dating can be perceived as a daunting task. It is imperative to engage in challenging

discussions and assert your boundaries. This approach will effectively deter individuals incompatible with you, safeguarding you from potentially entering into a detrimental relationship.

5. Focus on moving forward and centering attention on oneself.
Instead of striving to exert influence over a group, allocate that energy to self-care. Acquire proficiency in another field of expertise while prioritizing your personal interests and continuing with your leisure pursuits. Instead of using an application, endeavor to explore alternative methods of meeting individuals, such as participating in gatherings and social events that align with your interests. You will be pleasantly surprised by the abundance of new acquaintances you will encounter, and you may have the opportunity to find a partner who aligns with your preferences. Strive to embody the qualities you seek in others.

6. Endeavor to avoid pursuing individuals.

Strive to choose individuals who reciprocate your affections consistently. If someone lacks enthusiasm towards you, take it as an indication to redirect your efforts towards someone who is genuinely enthusiastic about you. The indifference displayed by someone should be considered as a signal to part ways, rather than as motivation to exert more efforts.

Additional strategies for achieving success in the dating realm
dating game

7. Engage in joint energy investment with your acquaintances.

This may appear illogical at first glance, yet cultivating meaningful relationships and establishing a robust support network will prove to be significantly beneficial for your mental well-being in the long term. The idiom that suggests unexpected encounters can lead to true romance likely holds some truth. Thus, I advise you to delete that dating application, abstain from any further attempts to enforce its use, and instead enjoy socializing with your companions; after all, one never knows who you may encounter along the journey.

8. When an individual openly communicates their preference for a casual endeavor, it is advisable to accept their statement without further interpretation.
This approach epitomizes a highly effective means of asserting dominance in the realm of dating. Make an effort to refrain from making excuses when someone explicitly states their disinterest in pursuing a relationship. Instead, evaluate individuals based on their demonstrated qualities rather than hypothetical improvements that may be made.

Pursuing a meeting with them and becoming immersed in a reverie in which you hope to influence their perspective is a futile endeavor. When someone informs you that they are not seeking a committed relationship, they are openly indicating that they are unable to provide what you are seeking. If your ultimate goal is to establish a relationship, it is highly probable that you will experience frustration after investing significant time with someone who is unattainable, instead of endeavoring to find a suitable match aligned with your relationship objective.

9. Establish your desires, requirements, dealbreakers, and warning signs in a relationship, and subsequently take responsibility for adhering to them.

Prior to commencing a romantic relationship, it is advisable to compile a comprehensive list of your steadfast principles or criteria. If you encounter an individual towards whom you may not initially feel an attraction, yet they align with the criteria, I suggest you take the initiative to explore a connection, granting them a chance. Many individuals often engage in relationships with individuals who are not compatible with them. By gaining an understanding of your major concerns, you can begin to recognize your underlying patterns in the process of seeking a suitable partner. This represents a substantial breakthrough that will undoubtedly revolutionize your approach to dating.

10. Discover the means to prioritize your own company above all other associations.

When we seek a relationship out of loneliness, it often stems from a place of uncertainty and an attempt to compensate for a perceived deficiency. Instead of engaging in romantic relationships due to feeling socially awkward and isolated, focus on personal growth and internal validation. Engage in self-care activities and explore strategies for overcoming depression. When we seek validation from external sources in order to fill a void within ourselves, it is highly likely that we will be tempted to disregard our instincts and concerns to avoid the fear of loneliness. Ultimately, the pursuit of romantic relationships remains vital in one's journey through life. The remaining outcome relies entirely on your actions.

When embarking on a romantic relationship, one may experience the sensation of time appearing to accelerate at an accelerated rate. In the span of time, you transition from mere dating to building a prolonged companionship. Given the rapidity of events, it becomes crucial to gain a profound understanding of oneself prior to commencing a relationship, to avoid being caught up in the tumult and inadvertently losing touch with one's own identity and objectives.

Simultaneously, it is of utmost importance to enter an organization as a well-rounded individual who can contribute to the overall stability of the relationship. This is because the present phase of life primarily revolves around the two of you. You must have an understanding of your preferred methods of communication, identify your areas of weakness, outline your strategies for financial management, and demonstrate a commitment to ongoing reflection and improvement.

Request help

Given that the preceding information appears to lack utility or has proven ineffective despite prolonged effort, it may be worth considering alternative approaches and strategies.

Occasionally, we encounter instances of negative examples that are likely beyond our awareness. Occasionally, this could be attributed to a challenging prior experience that we are endeavoring to avoid repeating. Alternatively, it could be the case that the perceptions surrounding love that we have unconsciously developed over time are impeding our progress.

Gaining an external perspective can prove to be a valuable strategy for obtaining alternative viewpoints. Moreover, in addition to this, diligently confronting any challenges you may encounter can greatly enhance your overall well-being.

Occasionally, cherished individuals exhibit an ability to serve in a remarkable manner - individuals you entrust with unwavering honesty. Alternatively, engaging in a discussion with a legal representative can prove to be an effective method of efficiently resolving any difficulties. Instructors possess an exceptional understanding of the typical challenges individuals encounter in finding love, and they are adept at helping you reflect upon any difficulties you may be facing by prompting you to contemplate what you perceive as difficult. They will refrain from making judgments and instead actively listen to you, while endeavoring to assist you in finding a viable path forward.

How To Get The Man Of Your Dreams

Have faith in the possibility of love for yourself, and acknowledge your deservingness of it, and you will ultimately draw it towards you.

Exercise caution when categorizing individuals.

Standards hold significance as they provide guidance in the pursuit of personal desires, yet it is crucial to refrain from imposing categorical labels on individuals in the quest for love. Consider the case of Lena.

She endured two highly exploitative relationships, which subsequently fostered a gradual sense of caution when contemplating resuming dating. The two individuals who perpetrated mistreatment towards her in previous instances were, in fact, affiliated with her religious congregation. Although she did not possess a fervently devout nature, she elucidated to me during our initial encounter the significance she ascribed to the presence of religious faith in others.

After a period of solitude, she encountered Scott, an individual of remarkable kindness and deference; he not only earned her trust as a confidant but swiftly emerged as an exceptional alliance. After the passage of four years, their relationship endures and continues to flourish, narrating a delightful tale of love. However, the caveat lies in the fact that Scott does not possess any religious beliefs whatsoever. In fact, he identifies as an atheist; however, it is important to note that this does not inherently equate to being immoral. Scott is the sole individual who has bestowed upon Lena the affectionate and blissful companionship she had been yearning for.

Both individuals held a mutual respect for one another's perspectives, and as Lena continued to acquire knowledge from Scott, her conviction grew that he was the ideal partner for her. An individual characterized by virtues of integrity, deference, and empathy towards others.

Had she classified him as "non-religious" or "atheist," she would have forfeited the opportunity to embrace the love of her existence.

When compiling your customary inventory, it is imperative to demonstrate authenticity concerning the significance of each item and the underlying reasons for its importance. The responses obtained will provide you with valuable guidance towards the correct course.

Distinguished individuals can be found in various hues, ethnic backgrounds, body types, and religious beliefs.

5. The Challenges and Remedies of Exercising High Standards when Selecting a Romantic Partner

Certain women claim, "I am excessively discerning," insinuating that such selectiveness is the cause behind their unmarried status.

I have encountered individuals of both genders who remain in pursuit of love and connection, exhibiting specific criteria that are incongruous with what they themselves can bring to the table. I designate this occurrence as a discrepancy in standards that are of an elevated nature.

I do not assert that maintaining high standards is detrimental or lacks significant rationale. It is illogical to lack awareness regarding one's own demands and offerings.

Certain criteria that individuals expect their ideal partners to possess may not align with their own identities, thereby rendering them irrelevant and nonsensical.

It is unsurprising that they were unable to locate a suitable business associate. It is highly likely that their romantic relationship would have already undergone a transformation had they been cognizant of the prescribed hierarchy of compatibility.

It appears to be a matter of general knowledge, yet regrettably, certain individuals possess a lack of awareness regarding this fact, resulting in their solitary, desolate, and perplexed state.

To exemplify the significance of being conscious of one's standards, let us examine the circumstances surrounding Miranda's situation.

She possessed exceedingly stringent criteria and aspired to be in a relationship with a male of exceptional caliber. One could describe her as having an unremarkable appearance, yet possessing considerable untapped potential that could be actualized through concerted efforts.

Now the predicament arises: how can she anticipate that a highly appealing gentleman would develop affection for her?

I am aware that in certain relationships, the woman may not possess the same level of physical attractiveness as her male counterpart. We are all aware of such cases, however, these couples present rare exceptions. Counting on one's life mirroring these exceptions is akin to placing a wager on a lottery. There is a possibility of occurrence, although the likelihood is quite low.

I will revert to my previous illustration involving Miranda, who aspired to encounter an individual of an exemplary stature, reminiscent of a top-tier model, with the desire to cultivate a profound and purposeful romantic connection. Miranda lacked self-assurance, encountered difficulties when engaging in conversations with men, and neglected her personal appearance in order to appeal to her high-profile partner in the modeling industry. How is it conceivable that she would anticipate the affections of an exceedingly appealing individual to grow for her in such a realm?

One potential resolution could be attained by aligning with her criteria. If she were to invest efforts in enhancing her confidence, refining her grooming, and cultivating her charm, she has the potential to exude noticeable attractiveness.

Conform to your own set of criteria, and you will draw the attention of the ideal partner. There is no need for you to alter your being. You simply need to draw forth the innate excellence within you. The concept is rather straightforward, as it already exists intrinsically within your being. Keep in mind that standards originate from within oneself.

The objective is not merely to acquire any man, or even a commendable man, but rather to find the man who will genuinely bring you happiness by aligning with your desired qualities and fulfilling your needs in life.

Would you like to inquire about his criteria?

There is no need for concern. He will promptly inform you in due course. When an individual discovers the object of their search, they are unable to conceal their satisfaction. He will respond affirmatively, either through verbal or nonverbal means.

If, for instance, his romantic preference inclines towards femininity, your expression of utmost femininity will undoubtedly elicit joy in him and be readily apparent. Similarly, if he finds appeal in androgynous qualities and you embody them adeptly, he will likewise find contentment.

Remain authentic to your own individuality, and you shall eventually encounter a compatible individual who shares parallel interests and preferences.

Despite assuming the role of a detective and diligently attempting to unravel his inner thoughts and desires, he alone possesses the exclusive knowledge of his feelings and aspirations. Attend to his spoken words and observe his nonverbal signals. Do not endeavor to conceive notions. If his interest does not appear sufficiently strong, it straightforwardly indicates that you do not meet the criteria set forth on his list.

Rest assured, he will promptly exhibit that. There is no requirement for you to inquire. However, adhering to the guidance provided in this book would ensure that you exclusively pursue relationships with individuals who seek compatibility with your authentic self.

If one were attempting to conform to his expectations in order to satisfy him, eventually he will discern that you do not embody the idealized woman he sought.

It is disheartening to observe that numerous men exploit women who demonstrate a willingness to conform to their preferred ideals in pursuit of a romantic connection.

Please be informed that a woman who is empowered possesses a partner who harbors profound affection for her. If his initial feelings of affection towards you begin to diminish and he displays signs of disengagement, it is advisable to refer to the corresponding chapters titled 'The Empowered Woman Principles' and 'Navigating His Withdrawal: Effective Strategies'.

Males are not in pursuit of flawlessness, neither are we. Each of us, whether knowingly or unknowingly, seeks to encounter the individual who aligns with the vision we hold dear, necessitating the establishment of personal criteria.

Do not anticipate that an individual will modify their standards on your behalf. Either you meet the criteria he has established for his life, or it would be advisable for you to seek a compatible partner elsewhere. Do not anticipate any individual to alter themselves solely for your benefit.

The aforementioned statement is also applicable to women. We should never alter our fundamental nature to accommodate a man in our midst. In the event that he does not meet your expectations, it would be prudent to redirect your efforts and commence your search for an exceptional individual in alternative contexts.

Strategies For Achieving Your Ideal Female Self

You now possess a significantly enhanced understanding of the type of relationship you desire. Taking that into consideration, you have crafted a more distinct and intricate depiction of the type of individual you are seeking, someone who shares your aspirations for a mutually desired partnership.

This is your dream. Please bear in mind this advice in order to avoid engaging with, or expending any further time on, an unsuitable individual. You are endeavoring to discontinue that behavior, which is why you are engaging in the exercises provided within this book.

In light of your aspiration, how adequately do you align with it? That is a query that may not typically enter your mind. May I inquire if you happen to be the individual this gentleman is in search of?

It might appear unconventional for you to transform into the embodiment of your ideal self, yet it aligns with the age-old adage that asserts one's capacity to harbor genuine affection for others and receive love in return is contingent upon one's self-acceptance and self-love."

One's demonstration of self-love influences and shapes the manner in which others perceive and love them. They learn from you. If an individual recurrently behaves in a disrespectful or unkind manner towards you, it is primarily due to your tolerance of such conduct. However, I am jumping ahead of the present circumstances. Please bear in mind the aforementioned information as you proceed with this section.

Due to your diligent engagement with this book, coupled with your active completion of the assignments, you belong to the minority of women who are actively assuming control over their lives. I commend you for that. The primary focus of this book, along with all the principles I impart, revolves around the idea of cultivating a genuine and authentic version of yourself.

By unveiling your authentic self, radiant and brilliant, you will exude the utmost allure. You will attract a broader demographic of gentlemen, who, as you cultivate your feminine qualities, will be inclined to establish a deeper acquaintance with you. Once you encounter that exceptional individual, Mr. Right, you are highly inclined to forge a genuine and enduring love that surpasses any prior encounters.

I am of the perspective that it is essential for you to strive towards attaining the utmost potential of your personal growth and development – striving to embody the idealized version of yourself, the embodiment of your aspirations. Engaging in this act will lead to an increase in your overall happiness, primarily due to your inherent qualities, which in turn will enhance your appeal to the male individuals you encounter.

The underlying objective is to assist you in discerning the necessary criteria for attracting a gentleman who possesses all the essential qualities desired in a relationship or partner, while simultaneously lacking the traits deemed intolerable in a male counterpart. In order to obtain the desired individual, it is imperative that he possesses a sense of attraction towards you. The greater your self-love and overall contentment with your identity and character, the more pronounced your radiance of femininity will be.

Let us commence undertaking this section promptly. I trust that due to your personal involvement, you will perceive this journey as captivating.

Step #1

As it has become apparent, I am a firm advocate of the immense significance of writing. This is due to the fact that writing provides the means to delve into aspects of one's inner self that may remain inaccessible through mere contemplation. This is precisely why the act of maintaining a journal holds such profound influence.

Now, as an initial task in this particular section, kindly provide a detailed portrayal of yourself in the manner that aligns with your envisioned ideal self. If you are already in a state of self-perception, kindly proceed to provide a detailed account of your current state.

Please provide an account of your physical attributes, cognitive abilities, sociability, interpersonal proficiencies, aptitude in intimate relationships, skills in managing a household, spiritual inclinations, creativity, and your capacity for humor—anything that you believe shapes your identity or that you aspire to embody.

- Commence the composition of your essay forthwith and derive enjoyment from the process.

What was your experience like, when composing the essay regarding your envisioned self? Did it provoke exhilaration, motivation, or perchance give rise to unease? Please proceed indoors, preferably engaging in a

Relaxation Meditation, and conscientiously reflect upon your emotional state.

• Record your personal realizations in your journal pertaining to self-discovery.

Upon reviewing your description, kindly compile a comprehensive inventory of your most notable attributes. These are the aspects that you hold in high regard when it comes to your own character. Essentially, you are extracting the distinctive aspects that define your individuality from the essay.

www.ingramcontent.com/pod-product-compliance
Lightning Source LLC
Chambersburg PA
CBHW050243120526
44590CB00016B/2192